SCHIRMER'S LIBRARY OF MUSICAL CLASSICS

Compositions for the Piano

FRÉDÉRIC CHOPIN

Edited, Revised, and Fingered by
RAFAEL JOSEFFY

Historical and Analytical Comments by
JAMES HUNEKER

ISBN 978-0-7935-5912-1

G. SCHIRMER, *Inc.*

DISTRIBUTED BY

7777 W. BLUEMOUND RD. P.O. BOX 13819 MILWAUKEE, WI 53213

THE MAZURKAS

I

DURING his lifetime Chopin published forty-one Mazurkas, in eleven cahiers of three, four, and five numbers. Opus 6, four Mazurkas, and opus 7, five Mazurkas, were published December, 1832; opus 17, four Mazurkas, May 4, 1834; opus 24, four Mazurkas, November, 1835; opus 30, four Mazurkas, December, 1837; opus 33, four Mazurkas, October, 1838; opus 41, four Mazurkas, December, 1840; opus 50, three Mazurkas, November, 1841; opus 56, three Mazurkas, August, 1844; opus 59, three Mazurkas, April, 1846 (no dedication); and opus 63, three Mazurkas, September, 1847. Besides these there are opus 67 and 68, published by Fontana after Chopin's death, consisting of eight Mazurkas, and there are miscellaneous numbers, two in A minor, both in the Kullak, Klindworth and Mikuli editions; one in F sharp major, said to have been written by Charles Mayer—in Klindworth—and four others in the keys of G, B flat, D, and C major, respectively. This makes fifty-five authentic specimens. Niecks thinks that there is a well-defined difference between the Mazurkas as far as opus 41 and those that follow. In the latter he misses "savage beauties," and spontaneity. As Chopin gripped the form, as he felt, suffered and knew more, his Mazurkas grew broader, revealed *Weltschmerz*, became elaborate and at times impersonal, but seldom lost the racial hue and "snap." They are like sonnets in their well-rounded mechanism and, as Schumann says, something new is to be found in each. Toward the last a few are blithe and jocund, but they are the exceptions. In the larger ones the universal quality is felt, but sometimes to the detriment of intimate Polish characteristics. These Mazurkas are precisely what they are named; only some dance with the heart, others with the heel. Comprising a large and original portion of Chopin's compositions, they are the least known. Perhaps when they wander from the map of Poland they lose a moiety of their native fragrance. Like hardy, simple, wild flowers they are mostly for the open air, the only out-of-door music Chopin ever made. But even in the open, and under the moon, the note of self-torture, of sophisticated sadness is not absent. Do not accuse Chopin, for this is the sign-manual of his race. The Pole suffers in song the joy of his sorrow.

The Mazurkas, said De Lenz, are the songs of Heinrich Heine on the piano. "Chopin was a phœnix of intimacy with the piano. In his Nocturnes, Mazurkas, he is unrivalled, downright fabulous." No compositions are so Chopinesque as the Mazurkas. Ironical, sad, sweet, joyous, morbid, splenetic, sane and dreamy, they illustrate what has been said of the composer—"his heart is sad, his mind is gay." That subtle quality, and for an Occidental enigmatic, which the Poles call *Zal*, is in some of the Mazurkas; in others the fun is almost uproarious. *Zal*, a poisonous word, is a baleful compound of pain, sadness, secret rancor and revolt. It is a Polish, a Slavic quality and it may be found also in the Celtic peoples. Oppressed nations with a tendency to lyricism develop this psychical secretion. Liszt writes that "the *Zal* colors with a reflection now argent, now ardent, the whole of Chopin's works." This sorrow is the very soil of Chopin's nature. He so confessed when questioned by Countess d'Agoult. Liszt further explains that the strange word *Zal* includes in its meaning "all the tenderness, all the humility of a regret borne with resignation and without a murmur"; it also signifies "excitement, agitation, rancor, revolt full of reproach, menace never ceasing to threaten if retaliation should ever become possible, feeding itself meanwhile with a bitter, if sterile hatred." Sterile, indeed, must be such a consuming passion. Even where his patriotism became a lyric cry, this *Zal* tainted the source of Chopin's joy; it made him irascible, and with his power of self-repression this smouldering, smothered rage must have well-nigh suffocated him, and in the end proved harmful alike to his nerves and art. As in certain phases of disease, it heightened the beauty of his later work, unhealthy, feverish as it is, withal beautiful. The pearl is said to be a morbid secretion; so the spiritual ferment *Zal* gave to his music its morbid beauty. It is in the B minor Scherzo, but not in the A flat Ballade. The F minor Ballade overflows with it, as does the F sharp minor Polonaise, but not the first Impromptu. Its dark introspection colors many of the Preludes and Mazurkas, and in the C sharp minor Scherzo it may be found in all its acrid flowering—truly *fleurs du mal*. It is the collective sorrow and tribal wrath of a downtrodden nation, and for that reason the Mazurkas have ethnical value. As concise, even as curt as the Preludes, they are for the most part highly polished; they are dancing preludes and often tiny single poems of poetic intensity and passionate plaint.

Absolutely Slavonic, though a local dance in the province of Mazovia, the Mazurek, Mazurka, is written in three-four time, with the usual displaced accent in music of Eastern origin. Brodzinski has said that in its primitive form the Mazurka is only a kind of Krakowiak, less lively, less *sautillant*. At its best it is a dancing anecdote, a story told in a charming variety of steps and gestures. It is intoxicating, rude, humorous, poetic, above all, melancholy. When he is happiest, he sings his saddest, does the Slav. Hence his predilection for minor modes. The Mazurka may be in three-four or three-eight time. Sometimes the accent is dotted, but this is by no means absolute. The scale is a mixture of major and minor—melodies are often encountered that grow out of a scale shorn of a degree. Occasionally the augmented second, the so-called Hungarian interval, is encountered, and skips of a third are of frequent occurrence. This, with progressions of augmented fourths and major sevenths, gives to the Chopin Mazurkas an exotic character apart from their novel and original content. As was the case with the Polonaise, Chopin took the framework of the national dance, developed it, enlarged it and hung upon it his choicest melodies, his most piquant harmonies. He breaks and varies rhythm in half a hundred ways, lifting to the poetic plane the original heavy-hoofed peasant dance. But in the process of this idealization he never robs it altogether of the flavor of the soil. It is all, in its wayward disguises, the Polish Mazurka, and according to Rubinstein is with the Polonaise the only Polish-reflective music Chopin has made; although "in all of his compositions we here rejoicingly relate of Poland's vanished greatness, singing, mourning, weeping over Poland's downfall, and all in the most beautiful, musical manner."

In addition to the "hard, inartistic modulations, the startling progressions and abrupt changes of mood" that jarred the old-fashioned Moscheles and dipped in vitriol the pen of Rellstab, there is also in the Mazurkas the greatest stumbling-block of all, the much exploited *tempo rubato*. Berlioz asserted that Chopin could not play in time—which was not true—and Meyerbeer believed likewise. "Chopin leans about freely within his bars," wrote an English critic; and what to the sensitive listener is a charming wavering and swaying in the measure is for the pedantic a rank departure from the time-beat. According to Liszt's description of the rubato, "a wind plays in the leaves, life unfolds and develops beneath them, but the tree remains the same—that is the Chopin *rubato*." Elsewhere, "a *tempo* agitated, broken, interrupted, a movement flexible yet at the same time abrupt, and vacillating as the fluctuating breath by which it is agitated." Chopin was more commonplace in his definition: "Supposing," he explained, "that a piece lasts a given number of minutes; it may take just as long to perform the whole, but in detail deviations may differ." The *tempo rubato* is probably as old as music itself. It is in Bach, it was practised by the old Italian singers. Mikuli said that no matter how free Chopin was in his treatment of the right hand in melody or arabesque, his left hand kept strict time. Charles Hallé, the pianist, tells us that once he proved Chopin to be playing four-four instead of three-four measure in a Mazurka and Chopin laughingly admitted that it was a national trait. Hallé adds that he was bewildered when he first heard Chopin play, for he did not believe such music could be represented by musical signs. Still, he holds that this style has been woefully exaggerated by pupils and imitators. But if a Bach fugue or a Beethoven sonata be played with metronomic rigidity, both lose their flavor. Naturally abhorring anything that would do violence to the structural side of this composition, Chopin was a martinet with his pupils if too much license in *tempo* was taken. His music demands the greatest lucidity in presentation and a certain elasticity of phrasing. Rhythm need not be distorted, nor should there be absurd and vulgar haltings, silly or explosive dynamics. Chopin sentimentalised is Chopin butchered. He loathed false sentiment, for a man whose taste was nurtured on the music of Bach and Mozart never could have indulged in jerky, exaggerated *tempi*, or in meaningless expression. The very balance and symmetry of the Chopin phraseology are internal; a flowing, curved, waving manner, never square or hard, is the best method of delivery, yet with every accent showing, like the supple muscles of an athlete beneath his skin. Without its skeleton a musical composition is flaccid, shapeless, weak and without character. Chopin's music exacts a marked rhythmic sense. His *rubato* is rhythm liberated from scholastic bonds, but it does not mean disorder; he must not be played lawlessly. With his accentual life topsy-turvied he becomes a caricature.

II

The F sharp minor Mazurka of opus 6 begins with the characteristic triplet that plays such a rôle in this dance-form. Here we find a Chopin fuller-fledged than in the Nocturnes and Variations, and probably because of the form. This Mazurka, first in order of publication, is melodious, slightly mournful, but of a genuine freshness. The third section with the *appoggiature* realizes a vivid vision of country couples determinedly dancing. Number 2 of this opus is seldom played. It, too, has "the native wood-note wild," with its dominant pedal-bass, its slight twang and its sweet-sad melody in C sharp minor; there is hearty delight in the major, and how natural it seems. In E, Number 3 is still on the village green, the boys and girls romping through the dance. We hear a drone-bass a favorite device of Chopin's—the chatter of the gossips, the bustle of a rural festival. The harmonization is rich, vital rhythmic life. But in the succeeding Mazurka, E flat minor, a different note is sounded. Its harmonies are closer and there is sorrow abroad; the incessant circling about one idea, as if obsessed by fixed grief, is employed here for the first, but not for the last, time by the composer.

Opus 7 drew attention to Chopin. It was this set that brought down the critical thunders of Rellstab, who wrote: "If Mr. Chopin had shown this composition to a master the latter would, it is to be hoped, have torn it and thrown it at his feet, which we hereby do, symbolically." The B flat major Mazurka which opens opus 7 is the best known of these dances. There is an expansive swing, a *laissez-aller* to this piece, with its air of elegance, that is alluring. The *rùbato* flourishes and at the close we hear the footing of the peasants. A jolly, reckless composition that makes one happy to be alive and dancing. The next, which begins in A minor, is as if danced over one's grave; a change to the major does not deceive, it is too heavy-hearted. Number 3, in F minor, with its rhythmic pronouncement at the start, brings us back to earth; guitar-like is the bass in its snapping resolution. The section that starts on the dominant of D flat is full of vigor and imagination; the left hand is given a solo. This Mazurka has the true ring. The following one, in A flat, is a sequence of moods. Its initial assertiveness soon melts into tenderer hues, and in the A major Episode we find much to ponder. Number 5, in C, consists of three lines. It is a sort of *coda* to the set and echoes lusty happiness; a silhouette with a marked profile.

Opus 17, Number 1, in B flat, is bold, chivalric; you fancy you hear the ring of the warrior's sabre. The peasant has vanished or else gapes through the open window as his master goes through the paces of the courtly dance. We encounter sequential chords of the seventh, and their use, rhythmically framed as they are, lends a line of sternness. Niecks thinks the second Mazurka might be called "The Request," so pathetic, playful and persuasive is it. In E minor, it has a plaintive, appealing quality; the G major part is pretty. In the last lines the passion mounts, but is never shrill. In certain editions, in the fifth and sixth bars there is no slur, but a slur on two notes of the same pitch does not always mean a tie with Chopin. The A flat Mazurka Number 3 is pessimistic, threatening, even irritable. Though in the key of E major the trio displays a relentless sort of humor. The return does not mend matters. A dark page! In A minor, the 4th is called by Szulc the "Little Jew." Szulc, who collected anecdotes about Chopin with the title "Fryderyk Szopen" (the Polish way of spelling the name), told the story to Kleczynski, and it strikes one as being both childish and commonplace. To be sure, this Mazurka is rather doleful and there is a triplet of interrogation (the poor little Polish Jew of the story always asks, "What was that?") standing sentinel at the fourth bar; but it is also in the last phrase. But what of that? For me the A minor Mazurka is despairing, and with its serpentine chromatics and apparently suspended close—on the chord of the sixth—creates an impression of morbid irresolution modulating into a desperate gayety. Its indeterminate tonality may account for the restless moods evoked. Opus 24 begins with the G minor Mazurka, a favorite because of its comparative freedom from technical difficulties. Although in the minor mode, there is mental tonic in the piece, with its exotic scale of the augmented second, and its hearty trio. In the next, in C, we find besides the cu ious content a mixture of tonalities, also Lydian and Mediæval church modes. Here the trio is Occidental. The entire dance leaves a vague impression of discontent, while the refrain recalls the songs of the Russian bargemen. These Mazurkas are all so capricious, so varied, and Chopin never played them twice alike. They are creatures of moods, melodic air-plants, swinging to the rhythm of any vagrant breeze. The metronome is for the teacher; but metronome and *rubato* for Chopin's Mazurkas are mutually exclusive. The third Mazurka of opus 24 is in A flat. It is not deep, but pleasing, a real dance with an ornamental *coda.* But the next! Here is a gem, a beautiful and exquisitely colored poem. In B flat minor the figuration is tropical, and when the major is reached and those glancing thirty-seconds so coyly assail us, we realize the charm of Chopin.

The C minor Mazurka is another of those beautiful melodies. What can I say in praise of the deepening feeling at the *con anima?* It is replete with pathos. As Schumann wrote: "Chopin did not make his appearance accompanied by an orchestral army . . . he possesses only a small cohort, but to him belongs every soul to the last hero." Eight lines is in this, yet it has almost endless meanings. Number 2, in B minor, is called by Kleczynski "The Cuckoo." It is sprightly and with the lilt of Mazovia, notwithstanding its subtle progressions. Number 3, in D flat, is all animation, brightness and a determination to stay out the dance. The alternate major-minor of the theme is truly Polish, while the graceful trio and canorous brilliancy make it a favored number. The ending is epigrammatic. It comes so suddenly upon us, our ears pealing with the minor mode, that its very abruptness is witty. One sees Chopin smiling mockingly as he wrote it. The fourth of this opus is in C sharp minor. The sharply cut rhythms and solid build of this work give it an ample, a massive character. It is one of the big Mazurkas, and the ending, harmonically raw as it is—consecutive fifths and sevenths—quite compasses its intended meaning.

Opus 33 is a popular set. It begins with one in G sharp minor, which is curt and rather depressing. The relief in B major is less real than it seems—on paper. Number 2, in D, is bustling, graceful and full of unrestrained vitality. Bright and not particularly profound, it has been arranged for voice by Viardot-Garcia and sung by Marcella Sembrich. The third in this opus is the one described by De Lenz as precipitating a quarrel between Meyerbeer and Chopin. The Russian writer christened it "The Epitaph of an Idea," which title is the epitaph of an epigram. Meyerbeer was wrong; it is not in two-four; though Chopin slurs the last beat, the three-four is nevertheless there. This Mazurka is only four lines long, as charming as the briefest of the Preludes in A major. The next Mazurka is a famous warhorse for public pianists. In B minor, it is charged with veiled coquetries, hazardous mood-transitions, smothered plaints and growling recitatives. The continual return of the theme has given rise to all manner of fanciful programmes, set to stories from Polish poets, none of them quite convincing. In C sharp minor, opus 46, is a Mazurka that is lovely. Its scale is exotic, its rhythm forceful, its tune a little saddened by life, but its courage never fails. The theme sounds persistently, in the middle voices, in the bass, and at the close in full harmonies, giving it a startling effect. Octaves take it up in profile until it vanishes. Here is the very apotheosis of rhythm. Number 2, in E minor, is at heart not very resolute. It was composed at Palma, so Niecks avers, when Chopin's health fully accounts for the depressed character of the dance—which is sad to the point of tears. Of opus 41 he wrote to Fontana from Nohant, in 1839: "You know I have four new Mazurkas; one from Palma in E minor, three from here in B, A flat and C sharp minor. They seem to me pretty, as the youngest children do when the parents grow old." Number 3 is a vigorous, sonorous dance; No. 4, in A flat, over which editors deviate in the serious matter of text, is for the concert room, and is allied to several of his gracious Waltzes. It is playful and decorative, but not deep in sentiment.

III

Opus 50, the first in G, is healthy and vivacious, good humor predominates. In some editions it closes *pianissimo.* Number 2 is a perfect specimen of the aristocratic Mazurka. In the key of A flat, the trio in D flat, the answering episode in B flat minor makes the grace of the return one to be shielded and treasured. De Lenz finds Bach-like influences and imitations in the following C sharp minor. The texture of this dance is finer spun than any we have encountered. Opus 56, in B, is elaborate from the start. There is decoration in the E flat *ritournelle* and one feels the absence of a compensating emotion despite the display of contrapuntal skill. Very virtuoso-like, yet not so intimate as some of the others. There is the peasant in the first bars of No. 2, in C, but the A minor and what follows soon disturbs the air of *bonhommie.* Theoretical ease is in the imitative passages. Chopin is now master of his tools. The third Mazurka of this opus is in C minor; it is quite long and does not arouse an impression of totality. With the exception of a short break in B major, it is composed with the head, not the heart. In its sturdy affirmation not unlike the one in C sharp minor, op. 41, is the next Mazurka in A minor, opus 59. But that Chopin did not repeat himself is an artistic miracle. This Mazurka, like the one that follows, has a dim resemblance to others, yet there is always a novel point of departure, a fresh harmony, a sudden melody, a subtle turn which takes us away from the familiar road, or an unexpected ending. The A flat Mazurka of this set seems but an amplification of the dance in the same key, opus 50, No. 2. The double-sixths and more complicated phraseology do not render the later superior to the earlier Mazurka, yet there is no gainsaying the fact that it is a noble composition. But the next in F sharp minor, despite its rather saturnine aspect, is stronger in interest, if not in workmanship. It lacks the "savage beauties" of the F sharp minor example in opus 6, but it is far loftier in conception and execution. The inevitable triplet appears in the third bar and is a hero throughout. There is charm. Read the close of the section in F sharp. And in the major it ends, the triplet fading away, a mere shadow, a turn on D sharp, a victor to the last. Chopin at the summit of his invention! Time and tune that seldom wait for man are here his bond-slaves. Pathos, delicacy, boldness, a measured melancholy and the art of a euphonious presentation of all these qualities, with many other factors, stamp this particular Mazurka a masterpiece.

Niecks believes there is a return of the early freshness and poetry in the last three Mazurkas, opus 63. Full of vitality is the first number. In B, it is sufficiently varied in figuration and rhythmic life to single it among its fellows. The next in F minor has a more elegiac ring. Brief and not difficult in matter or manner is this dance. The third, of winning beauty, is in C sharp minor, and surely a pendant to the famous Valse in a similar key. Slender in technical configuration, it contains a perfect canon in the octave. The four Mazurkas (posthumously published in 1855) that comprise opus 67 were composed at various dates. To the first in G, Klindworth affixes the year 1849. Niecks gives it a much earlier year, 1835. I fancy the latter is correct, as the piece sounds like a youthful effort; it is jolly and rather superficial. The next, in G, is familiar. It is pretty and its date is set down by Niecks as 1849, while Klindworth gives 1835. Here again Niecks is correct, though I suspect that Klindworth accidentally mixed his figures. Number 3, in C, was composed in 1835. On this both editor and biographer agree. It is certainly an effusion of no great value, though a good dancing tune. Number 4, A minor, of this opus, composed 1846, is more mature, but in no wise remarkable. Opus 68, the second of the Fontana set, was composed in 1830. The first, in C, is commonplace; the next, in A minor, composed in 1827, is much better, lighter, and well made; the third, in F (1830), is weak and trivial; and the fourth, in F minor (1849), is interesting because it is said, by Julius Fontana, to be the last composition of Chopin. He put it on paper a short time before his death, but was too ill to try it at the keyboard. It is morbid enough with its sickly insistence in phrase repetition, close harmonies, and wild departure—in A—from the first figure. It completes the gloomy and sardonic loop, but we wish, after playing this veritable song of the tomb, that we had parted from Chopin in health, not disease. This page is full of the premonitions of decay. Too weak and faltering to be febrile, Chopin is here a prematurely exhausted, debile young man. There are a few accents of forced gayety, but they are speedily swallowed in the mists of approaching dissolution—the dissolution of one of the most sensitive poets ever born. Here we may echo, without the savor of Liszt's condescension or the irony of De Lenz—"Pauvre Frédéric!"

Kullak, Klindworth and Mikuli include in their editions two Mazurkas in A minor. Neither one is impressive. One—date of composition unknown—is dedicated "à son ami Émile Gaillard"; the other first appeared in a musical publication of Schott about 1842 or 1843, according to Niecks. Of this set I prefer the former: it abounds in octaves and ends with a long trill. There is in the Klindworth edition a Mazurka, the last in the set, in the key of F sharp. It is so un-Chopinesque and artificial that the doubts of the pianist, Ernst Paur, were aroused as to its authenticity. On inquiry—Niecks quotes from the London "Musical Record," July 1, 1882—Paur discovered that the piece was identical with a Mazurka by Charles Mayer. Gotthard, the publisher of this alleged Chopin Mazurka, declared that he bought the manuscript from a Polish countess—possibly one of the half hundred in whose arms the composer died!—and that the lady had parted with the autograph of Chopin only because of her dire poverty. It is, of course, a clear case of forgery.

Of the early Mazurkas, in G, and B flat—dating from 1825; in D, composed in 1829-30, but remodelled in 1832; and in C, 1833, the last is the most characteristic. The one in G is of slight worth. The B flat example starts out with a phrase that recalls the A minor Mazurka, numbered 45 in the Breitkopf & Härtel edition. Early as is the date of its composition, this Mazurka in B flat is pretty. There are breadth and decision in the C major Mazurka. Recasting improved the Mazurka in D; its trio is lifted an octave and the doubling of notes throughout lends it more weight and richness.

"In the minor key laughs and cries the Slav," wrote Dr. J. Schucht in his monograph. Chopin in the Mazurkas reveals not only his nationality, but his own enigmatic and fascinating personality. Within the tremulous spaces of this miniature dance is enacted the play of the human soul, a soul that voices the revolt and sorrow of a dying race, of a dying poet. They are epigrammatic, fluctuating, bizarre and tender, these Mazurkas, and precise and vertiginous; and while other composers have written in this dance-form, yet to say Mazurka is to say Chopin.

James Huneker

Thematic Index.

a Mlle la Comtesse Pauline Plater

Quatre Mazurkas

Revised and fingered by
Rafael Joseffy

F. Chopin. Op. 6, No. 1

25503

ff
ff
ffz
ffz
rallent.
Tempo Iº
f
cresc.
dim.
legato
cresc.
p
pp
f
scherz.
fz
fz

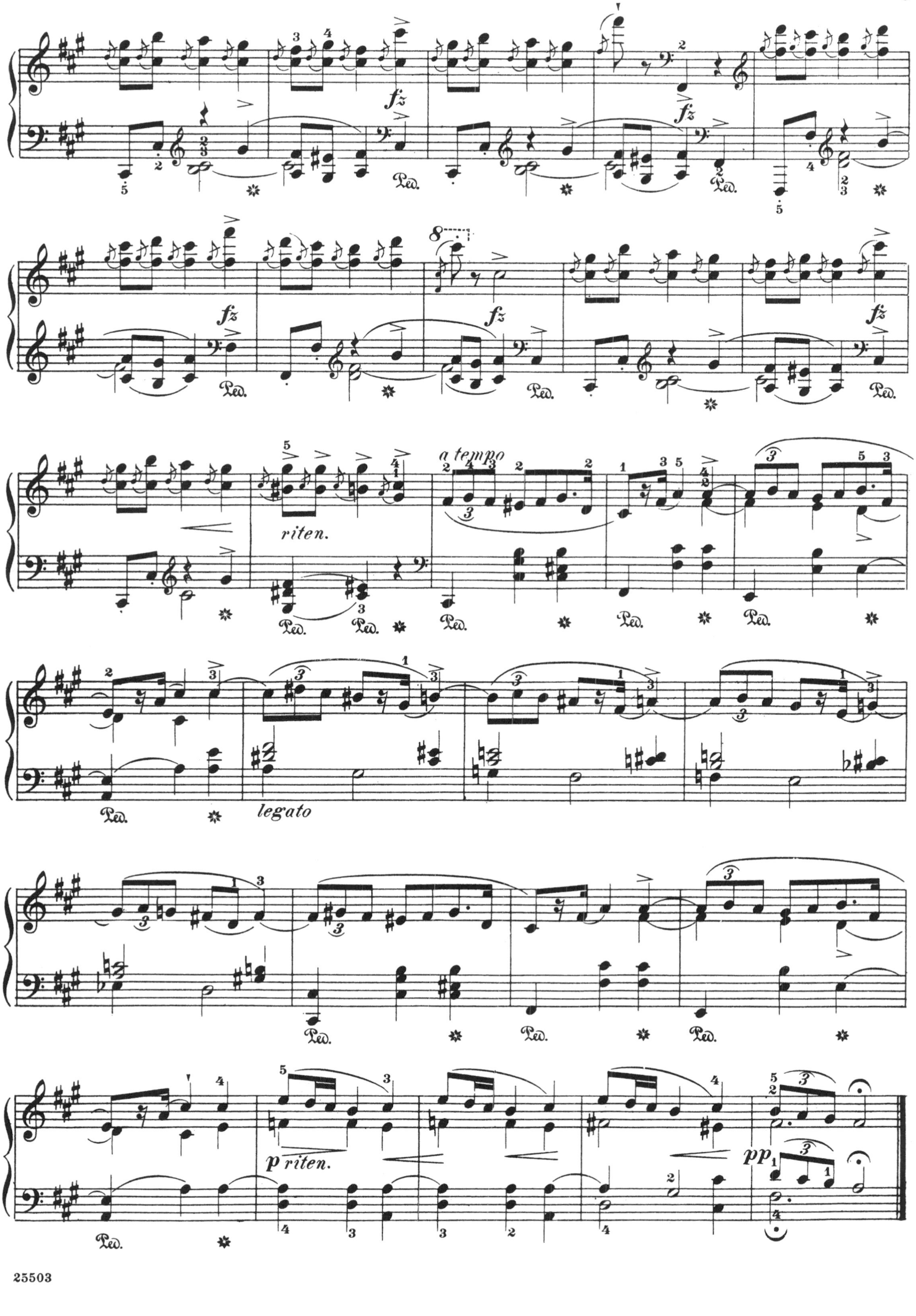

riten.

a tempo

legato

p riten.

pp

Mazurka

Revised and fingered by
Rafael Joseffy

F. Chopin. Op. 6, No. 2

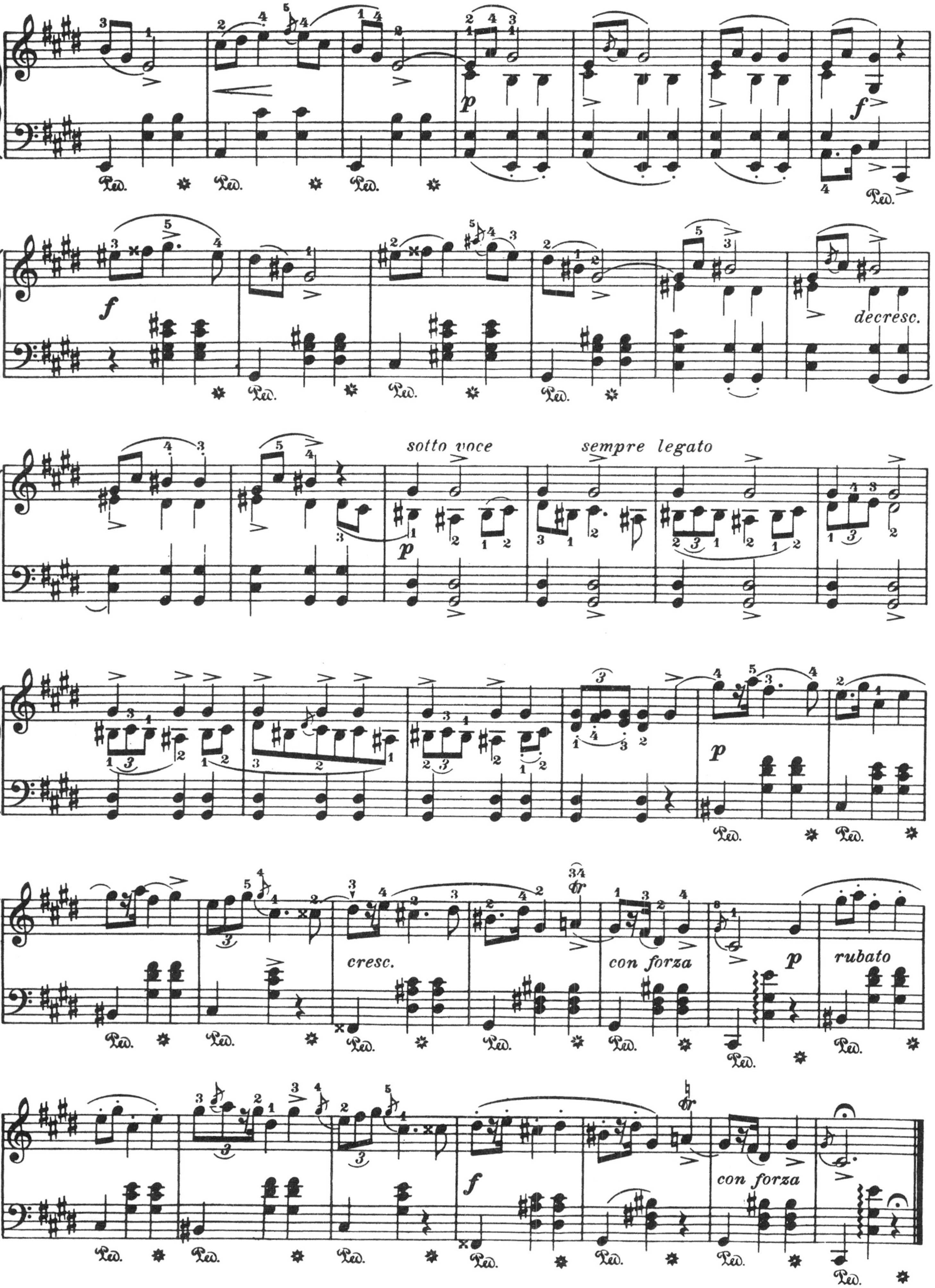

sotto voce

sempre legato

p

decresc.

f

cresc.

con forza

rubato

Mazurka

Revised and fingered by
Rafael Joseffy

F. Chopin. Op. 6, No. 3

ff
Ped.
p
cresc.
f
stretto dim.
risvegliato

p
Ped.
f
cresc.
decresc.
rit.
pp

Mazurka

Revised and fingered by
Rafael Joseffy

F. Chopin. Op. 6, No. 4

a Monsieur Johns de la Nouvelle-Orléans

Cinq Mazurkas

Revised and fingered by
Rafael Joseffy

F. Chopin Op. 7, No. 1

sotto voce
pp
Ped. ten.
rubato
a tempo
poco rall.
f
cresc.
Ped. come sopra
f
f
f

Revised and fingered by
Rafael Joseffy

Mazurka

F. Chopin. Op. 7, No. 2

Vivo, ma non troppo (♩ = 160)

6.

p

cresc.

f stretto

p

cresc.

poco rall.

a tempo

Fine

p

cresc.

a tempo
dolce
sempre legato
scherz.
f
fz
fz
riten.
a tempo
p dolce
scherz.

D. C. al Fine.

Mazurka

Revised and fingered by
Rafael Joseffy

F. Chopin. Op. 7, No. 3

ten.
Ped.
marcato
pp riten.
smorz.

pp
legato
Tempo Iº
f
con forza
rubato
p
pp

Mazurka

Revised and fingered by
Rafael Joseffy

F. Chopin. Op. 7, No. 4

25503

dolciss.
staccato
p riten.
sempre legato
molto rallent.
pp sotto voce
smorz.
a tempo
f
fz
p
f
sfz
f

Mazurka

Revised and fingered by
Rafael Joseffy

F. Chopin. Op. 7, No. 5

à Mlle Lina Freppa

Quatre Mazurkas

Revised and fingered by
Rafael Joseffy

F. Chopin. Op. 17, No. 1

dim.
Fine
dolce
dim.
D. C. al Fine

Revised and fingered by
Rafael Joseffy

Mazurka

F. Chopin. Op. 17, No. 2

stretto
pp
a tempo
f
p
riten.
8
Ped.

Revised and fingered by
Rafael Joseffy

Mazurka

F. Chopin. Op. 17, No.3

Fine
p
cresc.
dim.
smorz.
p
cresc.
cresc.
dim.
p
Dal segno al Fine

Mazurka

Revised and fingered by
Rafael Joseffy

F. Chopin. Op. 17, No. 4

p
Ped.
poco riten.
a tempo
ten.

dolce
p
ff
ten.

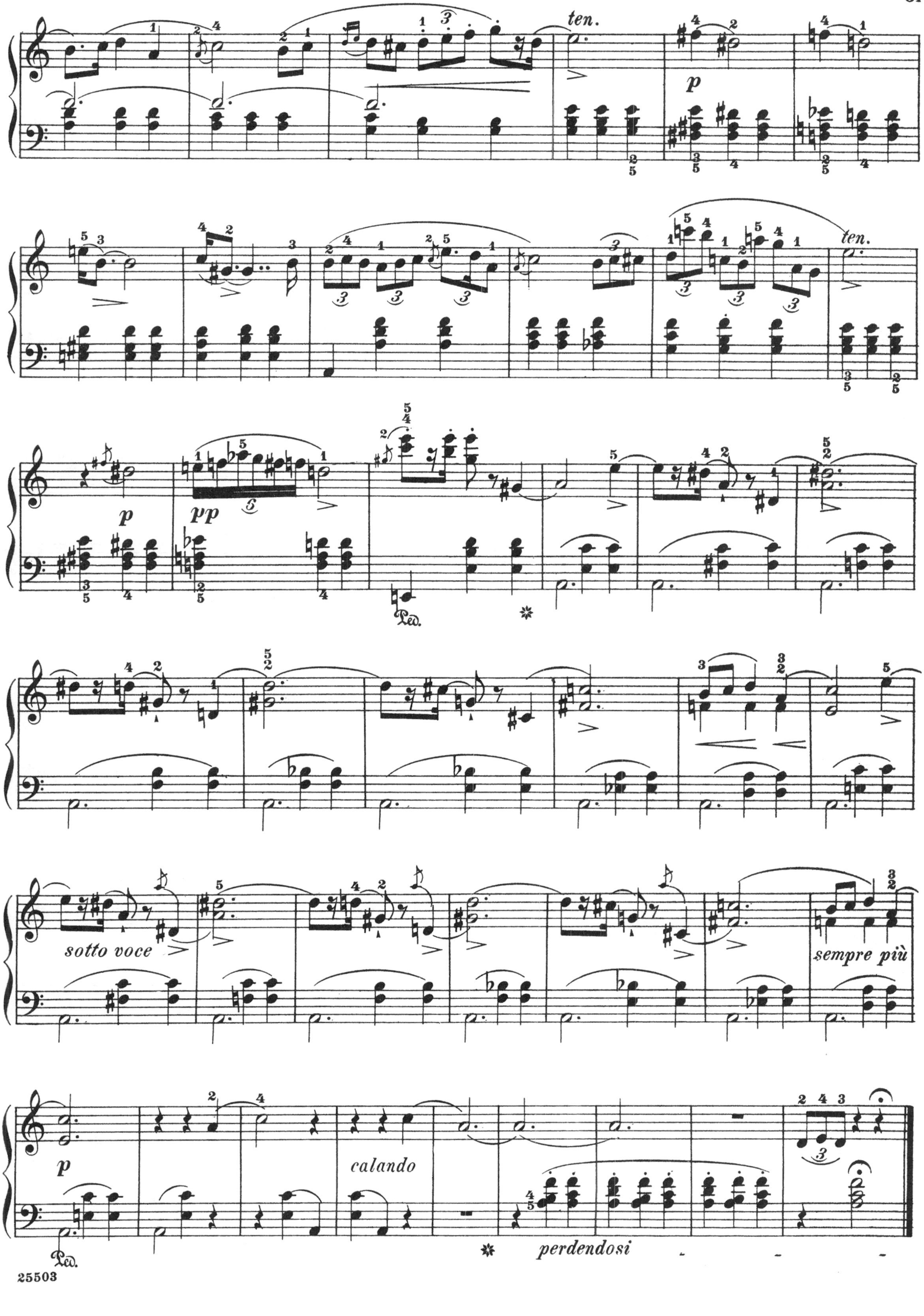

ten.

p

ten.

p

pp

sotto voce

sempre più

p

calando

perdendosi

à Mr. le Comte de Perthuis

Quatre Mazurkas

Revised and fingered by
Rafael Joseffy

F. Chopin. Op. 24, No. 1

con anima
a tempo
cresc.
riten.
dim.
sempre più p
riten.
pp

Revised and fingered by Rafael Joseffy

Mazurka

F. Chopin. Op. 24, No. 2

Printed in the U. S. A.

a tempo
riten.
più f
p
fz
pp
riten.

a tempo
dolce
sotto voce
poco riten.
sempre
p e legato

a tempo
pp sotto voce
pp
diminuendo sempre

Mazurka

Revised and fingered by
Rafael Joseffy

F. Chopin. Op. 24, No. 3

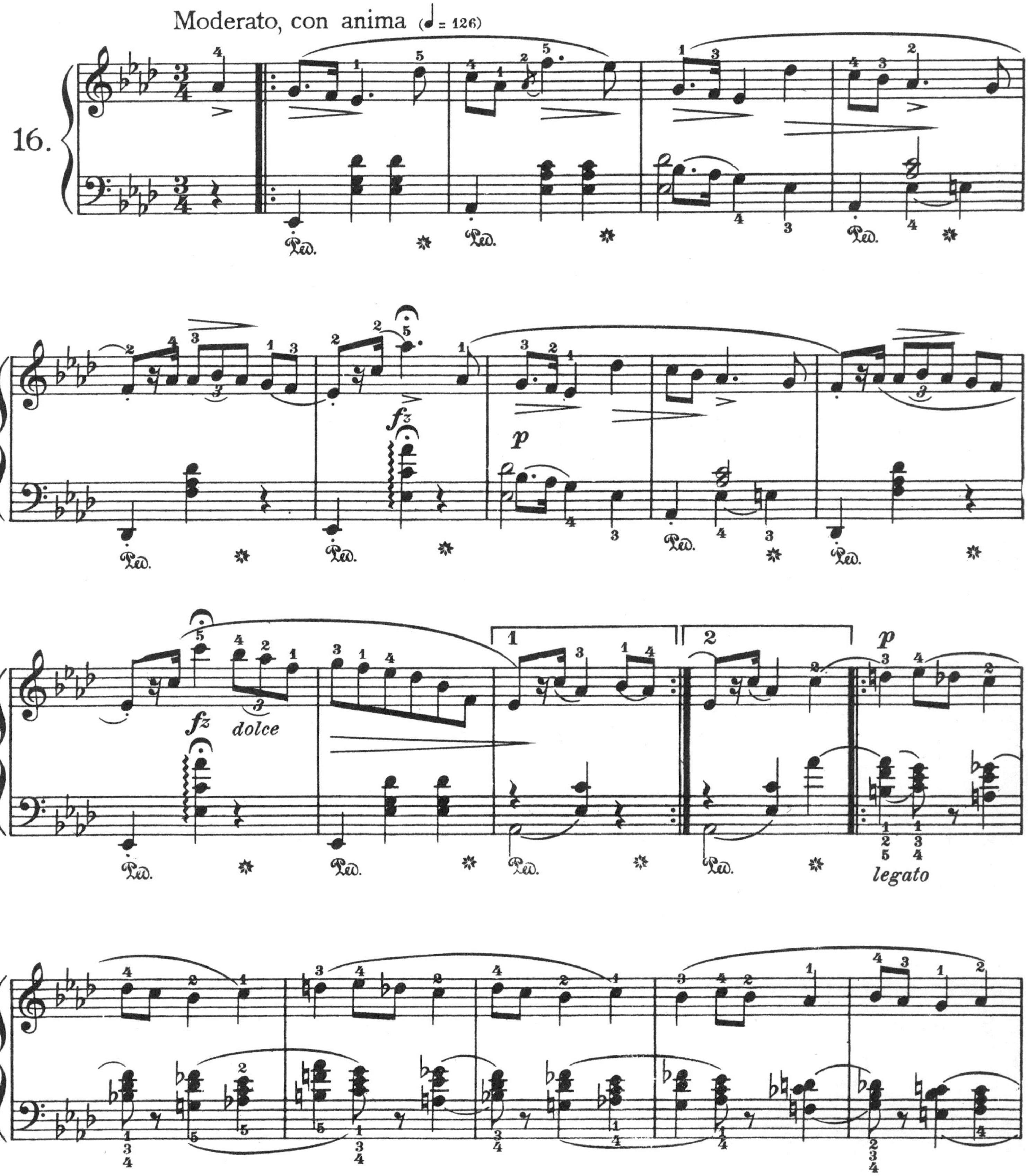

16.

Moderato, con anima (♩ = 126)

fz *p* *fz* *dolce* *p* *legato*

1 2

fz
p
fz
dolce
1.
2.
l.h.
dolciss.
perdendosi

Revised and fingered by
Rafael Joseffy

Mazurka

F. Chopin. Op. 24, No. 4

25503

accelerando, ritenuto
a tempo
cresc.
ff
p
più agitato e stretto
cresc.
ff
1.
2.
p
legato
sotto voce
1.
2.
con anima
f

pp
f
dolcissimo
pp
p
ritenuto
cresc.
a tempo
ff
pp
con forza
ff
sotto voce
cresc.
ff
dim.
accelerando
ritenuto
a tempo
p
Ped.

cresc.
ff
più agitato e stretto
cresc.
ff
p
riten.
calando
dim.
pp
pp
mancando
sempre rallent.
smorzando
pp
fz
p

à la Princesse de Würtemberg

Quatre Mazurkas

Revised and fingered by
Rafael Joseffy

F. Chopin. Op. 30, No. 1

dim.
poco riten.
a tempo
dim.

Revised and fingered by
Rafael Joseffy

Mazurka

F. Chopin. Op. 30, No. 2

p
p
poco cresc.
p poco a
poco
cresc.
fz

Revised and fingered by
Rafael Joseffy

Mazurka

F. Chopin. Op. 30, No. 3

25503

sotto voce
ben legato
cresc.

f
dim.
slentando
a tempo
risoluto
pp
ff

Revised and fingered by
Rafael Joseffy

Mazurka

F. Chopin. Op. 30, No. 4

21.

Allegretto

p legato

sotto voce

p

p
poco rit.
a tempo
sempre p
dim.
pp
f poco rit.
a tempo
sempre p

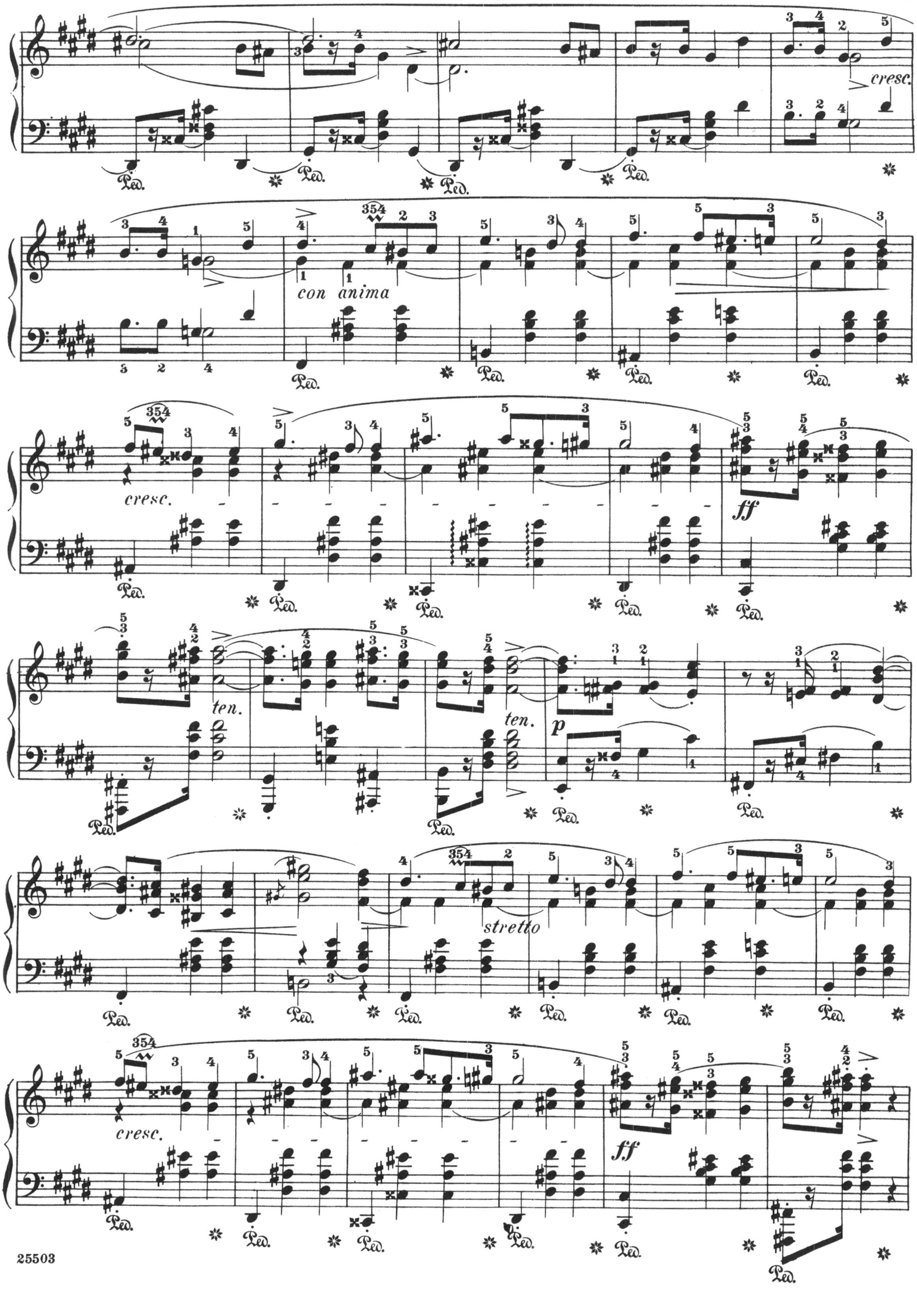

cresc.

con anima

cresc.

ff

ten.

ten.

p

stretto

cresc.

ff

p
dim.
p

Ped. Ped.

Ped. Ped.

p *poco stretto*

dim.

slentando

à Mlle la Comtesse Mostowska

Quatre Mazurkas

Revised and fingered by
Rafael Joseffy

F. Chopin. Op. 33, No. 1

p
dim.
f
p
dim.

58
Revised and fingered by
Rafael Joseffy
Mazurka
F. Chopin. Op. 33, No. 2
Vivace
23.
f
pp
Ped.
25503
Copyright, 1915, by G. Schirmer, Inc.

ff
pp
f
cresc.
fz
ff

f
1.
2.
f
pp
f
pp

ff
pp
accelerando
smorzando
8

Mazurka

Revised and fingered by
Rafael Joseffy

F. Chopin. Op. 33, No. 3

Ped.
Ped.
Ped.
Ped.
Ped.
Ped.

Mazurka

Revised and fingered by
Rafael Joseffy

F. Chopin. Op. 33, No. 4

25.

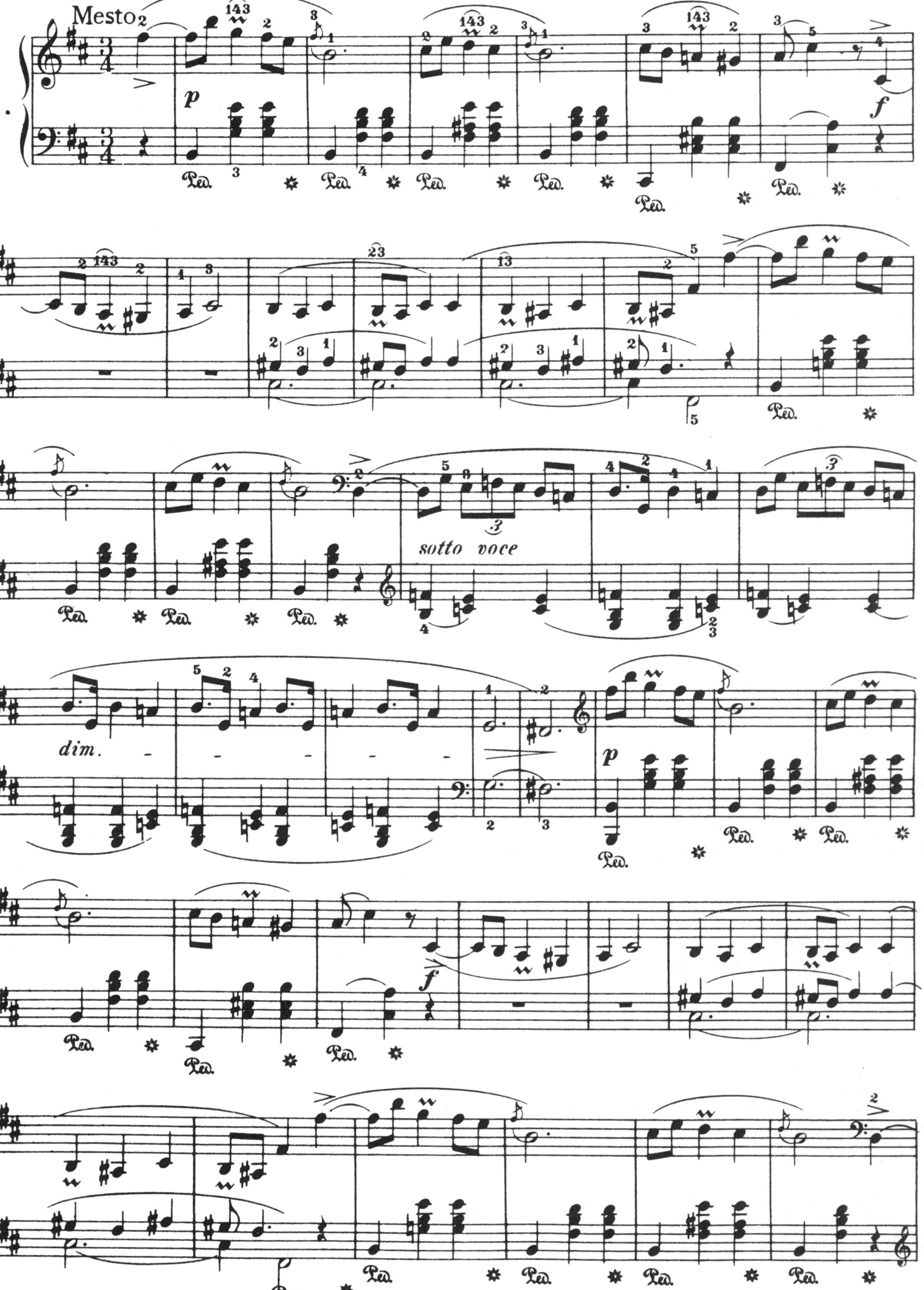

Mesto

p

f

sotto voce

dim.

p

f

sotto voce
dim.
f
fz
Ped.
p
sotto

voce
dim.
p
f
sotto voce
dim.
f

fz
p
fz
dolcissimo
p
fz
dolcissimo

f
Ped.
pp

poco rit.
p
f
sotto voce
dim.
dim.

à Mr. E. Witwicki

Quatre Mazurkas

Revised and fingered by
Rafael Joseffy

F. Chopin. Op. 41, No. 1

p
cresc.
Ped.
f
p
dimin.
cresc.
riten.

a tempo
pp
cresc.
f

cresc.
ff
p
pp
smorz.

Mazurka

Revised and fingered by
Rafael Joseffy

Andantino

F. Chopin. Op.41, No.2

27.

p f p f f

Ped. * Ped. * Ped. * Ped. * Ped. * Ped. * Ped. * Ped. * Ped. * Ped. * Ped. *

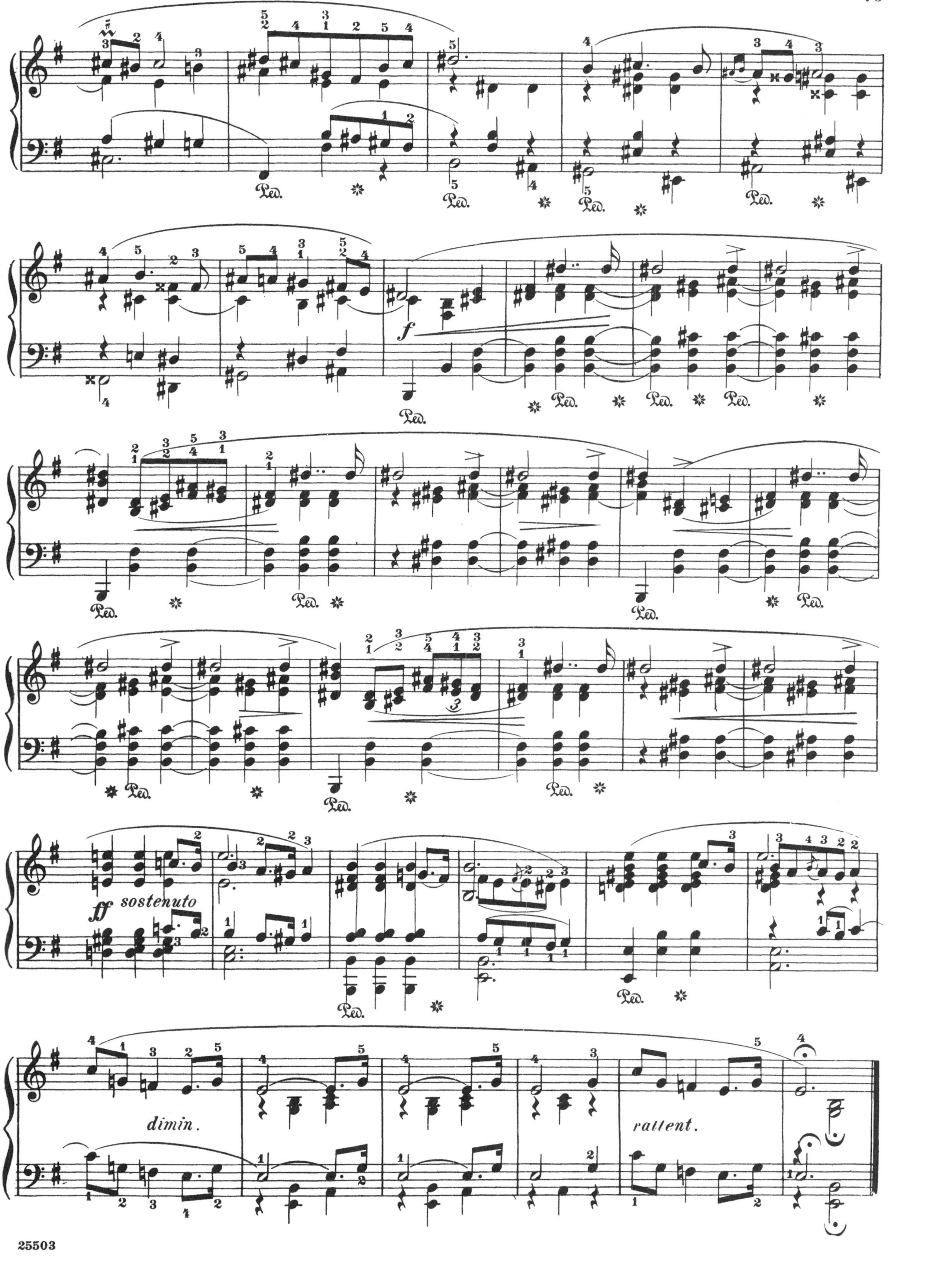

f

ff *sostenuto*

dimin.

rallent.

Revised and fingered by
Rafael Joseffy

Mazurka

F. Chopin. Op. 41, No. 3

28

cresc.
ff
sfz
fz
dimin.
p

Mazurka

Revised and fingered by
Rafael Joseffy

F. Chopin. Op. 41, No. 4

Allegretto

29.

dolce

Ped. * Ped. * Ped. * Ped. * Ped. * Ped. *

sotto voce
pp
f
dimin.

à Mr. Léon Szmitkowski

Trois Mazurkas

Revised and fingered by
Rafael Joseffy

F. Chopin. Op. 50, No. 1

fz
p
ten.

p
mf
fz

f
p sempre
ten
sempre diminuendo e riten.

Mazurka

25503

p
cresc.
p
rit.
cresc.
a tempo
fz

cresc.
p

Mazurka

Revised and fingered by
Rafael Joseffy

F. Chopin. Op. 50, No. 3

pp
p
sostenuto

f
p

cresc.
p
cresc.
f
dim.
p
pp
Ped.
slentando
ff

Revised and fingered by
Rafael Joseffy

à Mlle C. Maberly

Trois Mazurkas

F. Chopin. Op. 56, No. 1

Allegro non tanto

ritenuto
Poco più mosso
leggiero
p
sempre legato
poco rallent.

Tempo I°
p
cresc.
f
ritenuto
Poco più mosso
leggiero

Ped.
rallentando

Tempo I°
p
cresc.
f
p

Mazurka

Revised and fingered by
Rafael Joseffy

F. Chopin. Op. 56, No. 2

dolce
p legatissimo
poco ritenuto
a tempo
dim.

Mazurka
Revised and fingered by
Rafael Joseffy
F. Chopin. Op. 56, No. 3
Moderato
35.
mf
p
f
rall.
a tempo
25503
Printed in the U. S. A.
Copyright, 1915, by G. Schirmer, Inc.

f
p
dim.
f
f
p
cresc.

sempre legato
sostenuto

Ped.
legato
p
f
fz
p

f
p
Ped.
rallent.
a tempo

fz p
Ped.
dim.

Revised and fingered by Rafael Joseffy

Trois Mazurkas

F. Chopin. Op. 59, No. 1

sotto voce
cresc.
f
p

cresc.
f
f
p
ten.

Mazurka

Revised and fingered by
Rafael Joseffy

F. Chopin. Op. 59, No. 2

37.

p
mezza voce
fz
f
p

ff
fz
f
p
rall.
a tempo
pp

Revised and fingered by
Rafael Joseffy

Mazurka

F. Chopin. Op. 59, No. 3

38.

Vivace

f

cresc.

p

f

dim.
p
ri - te - nu -
to
a tempo

sf
p
f
ten.
dim.

cresc.
f
Ped.
dim.
p
riten.
a tempo
dim.
cresc.

f
dim.
p
accel.
dim.
a tempo
sostenuto
mf
fz

à Madame la Comtesse L. Czosnowska

Trois Mazurkas

Revised and fingered by
Rafael Joseffy

F. Chopin. Op. 63, No. 1

ten
dim.
p
f
p

f
p
dim.
fz
cresc.
fz
fz

fz
Ped.
dim.
pp
f

Revised and fingered by
Rafael Joseffy

Mazurka

F. Chopin. Op. 63, No. 2

Lento

40.

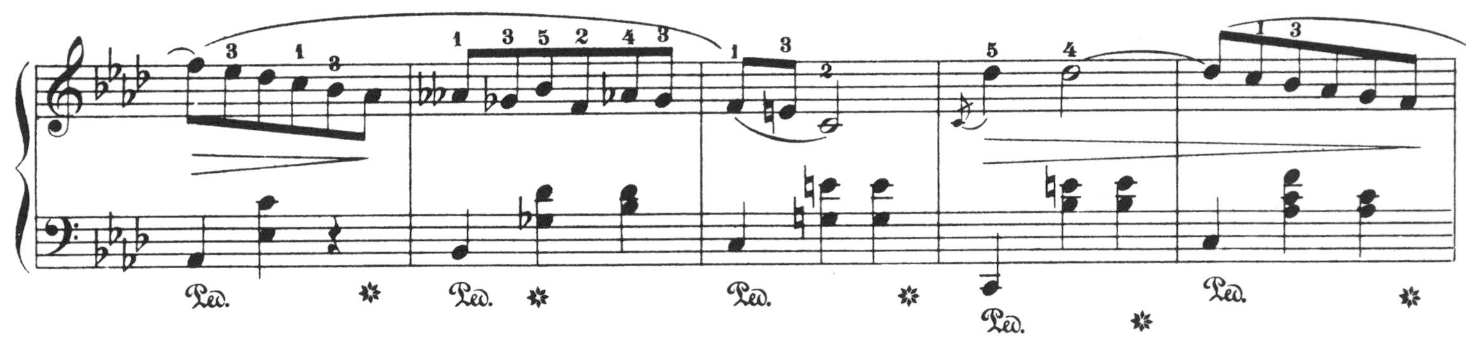

a tempo
f

Revised and fingered by
Rafael Joseffy

Mazurka

F. Chopin. Op. 63, No. 3

cresc.
ten.
p
(sopra)
f

Quatre Mazurkas

(Posthumous)

Revised and fingered by
Rafael Joseffy

F. Chopin. Op. 67, No. 1
(1835)

scherzando
marcato
riten.
a tempo
leggiero
cresc.

Mazurka

(Posthumous)

Revised and fingered by
Rafael Joseffy

F. Chopin. Op. 67, No. 2
(1849)

sf
Ped. simile
sf
p e legg.
p
sotto voce
poco cresc.
mf
Ped. come sopra
fz
sf
sf
f

Mazurka

(Posthumous)

Revised and fingered by
Rafael Joseffy

F. Chopin. Op. 67, No. 3
(1835)

cresc.
ff
poco rit.
a tempo
ten.
pp
riten.
a tempo
p
cresc.
ff
poco rit.

Mazurka
(Posthumous)
Revised and fingered by
Rafael Joseffy
F. Chopin. Op. 67, No. 4
(1836)
Moderato animato (♩ = 138)
45.
mf
marcato
riten.
a tempo
p
poco riten.
delicatiss.
a tempo
cresc.
dim.
legatissimo
1.
2.
cresc.

a tempo
rit.
cresc.
f
p
mf
Ped. come sopra
marcato
riten.
a tempo
cresc.
dim.
legatissimo

Quatre Mazurkas

(Posthumous)

Revised and fingered by
Rafael Joseffy

F. Chopin Op. 68, No. 1
(1830)

cresc.

Mazurka

(Posthumous)

Revised and fingered by
Rafael Joseffy

F. Chopin. Op. 68, No. 2
(1827)

mf
pp
legatissimo
poco a poco riten.
Tempo I°
Ped. come sopra
rit.
a tempo

Mazurka

(Posthumous)
Revised and fingered by
Rafael Joseffy
F. Chopin. Op. 68, No. 3
(1830)
Allegro, ma non troppo (♩ = 132)
48.
f
p
Ped. simile
ff
sf
p
Ped. simile
sf
p

Poco più vivo
Ped. ten.
p
riten.
Tempo I°
f
Ped. come sopra
p

Mazurka

(Posthumous)

Revised and fingered by
Rafael Joseffy

F. Chopin. Op. 68, No. 4
(1849) Last Composition

Andantino (♩ = 126)

49.

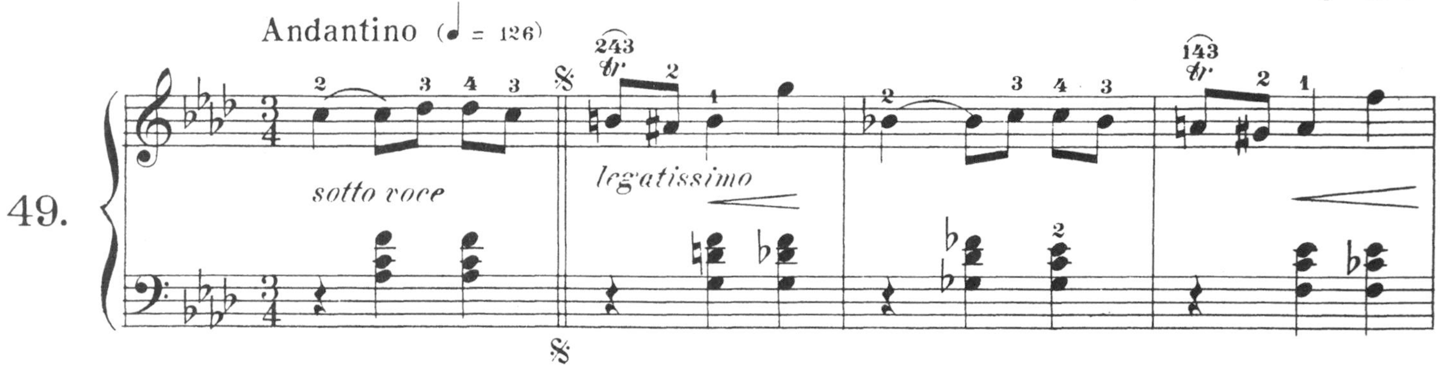

(Fine)
mf
pp
sempre legato
Dal segno senza fine

Mazurka

Revised and fingered by
Rafael Joseffy

F. Chopin

Allegretto

50.

p

poco cresc.

p

p

p
dim.
dim.
p

poco cresc.

à son ami Émile Gaillard

Mazurka

Revised and fingered by
Rafael Joseffy

F. Chopin

51.

25503

p
cresc.
p

legato
f